SACRED SOL HEALING INSTITUTE®

Foundational Personal Social Development

Mental Health Resilience

The Deconstructing Trauma™ Interactive Workbook Curriculum Focuses on ASAM Dimensions 3-6 and Co-occurring Conditions.

Physical, Mental, Emotional, and Spiritual Wellness

FROM SACRED SOL HEALING INSTITUTE
RENEE FRYE

The information used in this interactive curriculum comes from our Deconstructing Trauma Guidebook.

We have built it out into an interactive curriculum based on best practices for professionals, clients, and the general public.

See more at: www.sacredsolhealing.com

BONUS: Download our full-size, color pdf, "Deconstructing Trauma Toolkit," at https://deconstructing-trauma.com/. This is a complimentary gift for you.

Our Toolkit combines all the tools that have been offered throughout the Deconstructing Trauma Guidebook in one convenient reference space, plus bonus material.

Foundational Personal Social Development
Deconstructing Trauma™ Interactive Workbook Curriculum

Copyright © 2024. Renee Frye.

All rights reserved. No part of this publication may be reproduced, distributed, or transmitted in any form or by any means, including photocopying, recording, or other electronic or mechanical methods, without the prior written permission of the copyright holder, except in the case of brief quotations embodied in critical reviews and certain other noncommercial uses permitted by copyright law.

ISBN: 979-8-9896548-9-5

Book Production by Transcendent Publishing

Printed in the United States of America.

DECONSTRUCTING TRAUMA
in Our Daily Lives

The Deconstructing Trauma program teaches us a healing-centered life approach, allowing us to safely peel back the layers of trauma that have occurred throughout our lives. By deconstructing our past trauma, we can learn to safely navigate our mental, physical, and spiritual well-being.

Our curriculum is based on positive social development; through this process, behaviors, perspectives, and attitudes are learned, offering long-term positive changes in relationships and interactions involving oneself, peers, and family. As we learn to release negative and unhealthy behaviors that have manifested from our trauma, we are able to reprogram to positive mindsets and healthy behaviors.

Our program includes insightful daily awareness tools, mindful behavior modification strategies, a revolutionary positive behavior resilience method, and energy healing therapy. The combination of these specific approaches has a significant impact on the release of trauma, chaos, pain, and negativity.

WHAT YOU WILL LEARN

- Trauma and Addictions
- Triggers and Coping Strategies
- Identifying Negative Beliefs
- Emotional Regulation
- Mind-Body Awareness
- Self-Compassion
- Healthy Relationships
- Healthy Routines
- Balanced Life Wellness
- Healing-Center Life Approach

Name:

Date:

OVERVIEW

DECONSTRUCTING TRAUMA IN PERSONAL SOCIAL DEVELOPMENT

The Deconstructing Trauma Program: Healing Through Understanding

Trauma is a deeply ingrained aspect of human experience, affecting individuals in various ways and permeating every aspect of their lives. The Deconstructing Trauma program offers a unique approach to healing, focusing on understanding and addressing past traumas to foster mental, physical, and spiritual well-being.

Introduction to the Deconstructing Trauma Program

The Deconstructing Trauma program is designed to provide individuals with a healing-centered approach to addressing past traumas. Unlike other methods, which may focus solely on symptom management, this program emphasizes understanding the root causes of trauma and empowering individuals to navigate their healing journey safely.

Understanding Trauma

<u>Types of Trauma:</u> Trauma comes in many forms, ranging from emotional and psychological trauma to physical and environmental trauma.

<u>Effects of Trauma:</u> The effects of trauma can be far-reaching, impacting every aspect of an individual's life. From debilitating anxiety and depression to post-traumatic stress disorder (PTSD) and strained relationships, trauma can manifest in numerous ways, hindering one's ability to lead a fulfilling life.

Healing-Centered Life Approach

The Deconstructing Trauma program adopts a healing-centered life approach, prioritizing safe exploration and healing of past traumas. By creating a supportive environment conducive to healing, individuals are encouraged to confront their trauma and reclaim their sense of self.

Components of the Deconstructing Trauma Program

Insightful Daily Awareness Tools: Participants in the program are provided with daily awareness tools designed to increase self-awareness and mindfulness in their daily lives. These tools help individuals recognize triggers and patterns related to their trauma, empowering them to navigate their healing journey with greater insight.

Mindful Behavior Modification Strategies: Through mindful behavior modification strategies, individuals learn to cultivate awareness of their thoughts and behaviors. By practicing mindfulness and self-reflection, participants can identify and address negative patterns that may be perpetuating their trauma.

Positive Behavior Resilience Method: The program incorporates a revolutionary positive behavior resilience method aimed at building resilience and fostering positive behavior patterns. By focusing on strengths rather than weaknesses, individuals can cultivate a mindset of growth and empowerment.

Energy Healing Therapy: Energy healing therapy is integrated into the program to facilitate the release of trauma and restore balance to the body and mind. Through various energy healing techniques, individuals can address energetic blockages and promote healing on a holistic level.

Positive Social Development: Central to the Deconstructing Trauma program is the promotion of positive social development. By reshaping behaviors, perspectives, and attitudes, individuals can cultivate healthier relationships and interactions with themselves and others.

Releasing Negative Behaviors: One of the key objectives of the program is to help individuals release negative and unhealthy behaviors that have manifested as a result of their trauma. By addressing these behaviors at their core, individuals can break free from cycles of self-destructive patterns.

Reprogramming to Positive Mindsets: Through various techniques and exercises, participants learn to reprogram their minds to adopt positive outlooks and behaviors. By challenging negative thought patterns and replacing them with empowering beliefs, individuals can create lasting change in their lives.

Long-Term Positive Changes: The holistic approach of the Deconstructing Trauma program facilitates long-term positive changes in participants' lives. By addressing trauma at its root and providing tools for ongoing self-care and growth, individuals can experience profound transformation and healing.

Impact on Relationships and Interactions: As individuals progress through the program, they gain insight into their trauma and learn healthier coping mechanisms. This allows them to cultivate deeper connections and more fulfilling and healthy relationships.

Conclusion

The Deconstructing Trauma program offers a transformative approach to healing, allowing individuals to safely peel back the layers of trauma that have accumulated throughout their lives. Through a combination of insightful awareness tools, mindful behavior modification strategies, positive behavior resilience methods, and energy healing therapy, participants can release trauma and negativity, paving the way for lasting positive changes in their lives.

TRAUMA CAN LEAD TO ADDICTIONS

Trauma and substance abuse are interconnected issues that often coexist, creating a complex and challenging situation for individuals affected. Trauma refers to experiences that are emotionally distressing and overwhelming, often leaving a lasting impact on a person's physical, spiritual, mental and emotional well-being.

Substance use disorder is the repeated harmful use of any substance, including drugs and alcohol. The relationship between trauma and substance abuse is common. People who have experienced trauma may turn to substances as a way to cope with the emotional pain, numb difficult feelings, or attempt to regain a sense of control. Conversely, substance abuse can increase the risk of experiencing traumatic events, as it may lead to impaired judgment, risky behaviors, and involvement in dangerous situations.

TRAUMA IMPACTS ALL ASPECTS

In the chart, list the impacts of trauma in each area of your life.

Emotional Impacts	Social Impacts	Occupational Impacts	Intellectual Impacts

Financial Impacts	Spiritual Impacts	Physical Impacts	Environmental Impacts

THE ACES STUDY AND ITS IMPACT

Adverse childhood experiences (ACEs) can have a significant impact on the outcome of an individual's life. Potentially stressful events that may occur during childhood (0-17 years) are known as adverse childhood experiences (ACEs).

ACEs can have long-term detrimental repercussions on health, well-being, and life chances such as education and employment. These factors may increase the risk of injury, sexually transmitted infections, personal physical and mental health challenges, teen pregnancy, pregnancy issues, fetal death, sex trafficking, cancer, diabetes, heart disease, or suicide.

Our future doesn't have to be determined by our past. We can use this knowledge to seek change and resolve our past and present trauma. Trauma therapists, medical practitioners, holistic practitioners, and metal health professionals are all good resources! Your healing journey can begin here!

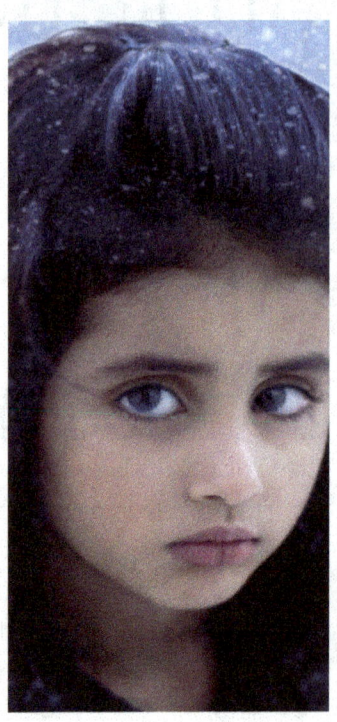

THE ACES SURVEY

Your ACEs (Adverse Childhood Experiences) Test: Before the age of 18 did you experience any of the following in the home you grew up in?
Mark the boxes of each questions below if it was part of your experience.

☐ 1. Household substance abuse: drinking, drugs, or prescription drugs?
☐ 2. Loss of parent/guardian through divorce, abandonment, death, or other reason?
☐ 3. Household members depressed, mentally ill, or attempted suicide?
☐ 4. Household adult violence: physical altercations, or threats to harm each other?
☐ 5. Household criminal behavior, and or incarceration, jail or prison?
☐ 6. Did you experience emotional neglect?
☐ 7. Did you experience physically neglect?
☐ 8. Did you experience emotional abuse?
☐ 9. Did you experience sexual abuse?
☐ 10. Did you experience physical abuse?

_____ Total Score of ACEs test above. Score will be a number 1 through 10 *

DECONSTRUCTING TRAUMA | FOUNDATIONAL DEVELOPMENT

Deconstructing Trauma Timeline

This is a trauma timeline to support you in recognizing, processing, and deconstructing critical traumatic events in your life. Make a list of the event(s), the date(s), and your physical and emotional reactions to each one, as well as what could help you heal. This can help you understand how these events have affected you and how to heal from them.

Traumatic Event	Date	Physical Reaction	Emotional Reaction	What Will Help Heal

List Your Negative Beliefs & How That Belief Makes You Feel.

Rate 1-10 Intensity

Rephrase Each Negative Belief Into a Positive Belief & List How The Positive Belief Makes You Feel.

Rate 1-10 Intensity

CHANGE NEGATIVE BEHAVIOR PATTERNS

With these "POSITIVE REPHRASING STEPS"

1. GAIN AWARENESS

Awareness allows you to interpret your actions, emotions, and thoughts without feeling bad about yourself. Negative thinking makes you feel bad about the world, yourself, and the future. It contributes to low self-worth, trauma, and addiction, making you feel like you're not effective in the world. Negativity is poisonous and creates a toxic cycle.

2. IDENTIFY TRIGGERS

A trigger is a stimulus that can bring back an unpleasant memory, emotion, or symptom. Triggers are important because, as we begin to recognize what affects us in our daily lives, we are able to mitigate, or lessen, negativity, pain, addiction, and trauma. A trigger can be resolved through dedication and work.

3. UNDERSTAND TRAUMA CYCLES

We all have trauma because we have had negative experiences in our lives. We project our own traumatic experiences, behaviors, and ideas onto others to keep ourselves safe. We develop false identities, false realities, and false scenarios, seeking safety. "Trauma-Related Expectations" create immediate and long-term toxic effects.

4. MEET BASIC NEEDS

If our basic needs have not been met, we will struggle to have a healthy, happy, safe, and fulfilled life. When we begin to meet our basic needs, we can start to heal from our trauma and be successful in our life recovery. Meeting our basic needs is not a one-and-done; it is an ever-changing, fluid life experience. Our needs will continue to change as our daily environment changes.

5. CREATE HEALTHY HABITS

Healthy habits create healthy lives. When we focus on communication skills, social skills, and self-management skills, we are able to strengthen our vulnerabilities by understanding and reducing triggers. By reinforcing a positive environment and positive, healthy habits, we reprogram the brain to release damage and reset itself, creating a different storage system for memories.

6. TRAUMA RECOVERY WELLNESS PLAN

We are not our trauma; it is a challenge for us to learn from and grow. We don't have to act on our impulses; we can observe them, discover where they come from, and allow them to inspire us to change. When we resolve the trauma surrounding them, we gain balance and peace. Creating a wellness plan allows us to live happy, healthy lives, free of addiction and past trauma, through a trauma-responsive wellness approach.

www.sacredsolhealing.com

© 2023 Sacred Sol Healing Institute® Trauma-Responsive Holistic Resources. All Rights Reserved.

List three negative behavior patterns and how you can change them using the "Positive Rephrasing Steps."

1.

2.

3.

If Our Basic Needs Have Not Been Met, We Will Struggle To Have A Healthy, Happy, Safe, And Fulfilled Life.

Maslow's Hierarchy Of Needs

Lack of our basic needs being met (food, shelter, transportation, clothes, clean water, education, mental and physical health, and access to quality health care) can lead to addictions, pain, trauma, and suffering. Mental, emotional, physical, and spiritual health challenges include depressive states, anxiety, toxic stress, insomnia, anger, hopelessness, despair, unhealthy relationships, suicide, and more.

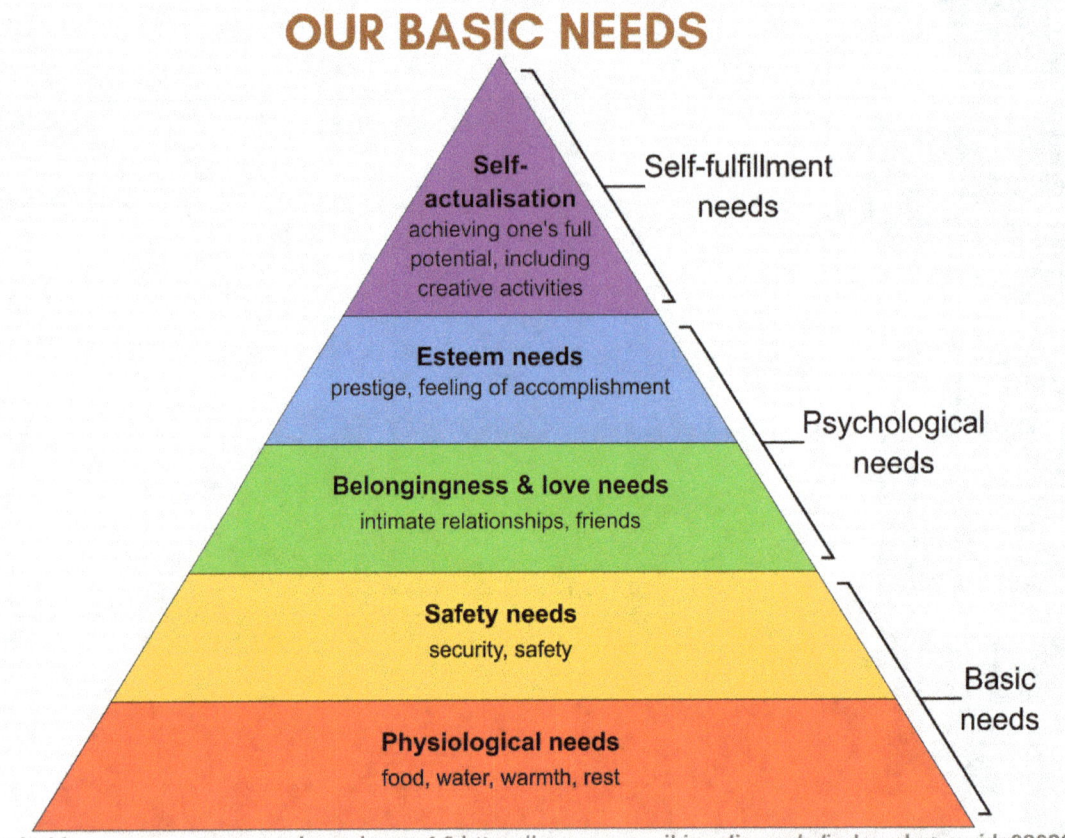

By androidmarsexpress own work, c c by-sa 4.0 https://commons.wikimedia.org/w/index.php>curid=93026655

When we begin to meet our basic needs, we can start to heal from our trauma and be successful in our life recovery. Meeting our basic needs is not a one-and-done; it is an ever-changing, fluid life experience.
Our needs will continue to change as our daily environment changes.

HIERARCHY OF NEEDS

Instructions: Describe an example of a need you have for each of the categories below: What makes me feel....

What makes me feel...

Fufilled
_____
_____

Confident
_____
_____

Loved
_____
_____

Safe
_____
_____

Good in my body
_____
_____
_____

DECONSTRUCTING TRAUMA | FOUNDATIONAL DEVELOPMENT

BASIC NEEDS DISCOVERY - LIST YOUR CURRENT LIFESTYLE

AM I MEETING MY BASIC NEEDS?

Rate 1-10

FOOD, WATER, SHELTER, REST

SECURITY, EMPLOYMENT, HEALTH

INTIMATE RELATIONSHIPS, FRIENDSHIPS

FEELING ACCOMPLISHED

ACHIEVING FULL POTENTIAL

WHAT I AM DOING GOOD

PLAN TO MEET MY UNMET NEEDS

DAILY TRIGGERS- LEARNED BEHAVIOR

A trigger, also known as a stressor, is an event or circumstance that may result in a negative emotional response. A trigger is a stimulus that can bring back an unpleasant memory, emotion, or symptom.

A physical trigger response can be heavy breathing, jaw clenching, upset stomach, trembling, chest pain, dizziness, crying, and sweating. An emotional trigger response can be anger, hurt, overwhelmed, powerlessness, helplessness, fear, anxiousness, sadness, unloved, weakness, and pain.

Tackling these emotions can be incredibly challenging and can have serious consequences for our mental health. The consequences of a person's emotional reaction to something can range from mildly disruptive to extremely dangerous, such as acts of violence.

As we learn to recognize our daily triggers, we can decrease negativity, suffering, addiction, and trauma. Resolving triggers and negativity brings balance, happiness, and peace.

COPING STRATEGIES
Ways to deal with triggers

- **Become aware of unhealthy coping skills**
  -Substance abuse, violence, depression...
- **Learn to recognize the trigger**
  -Anger, body shaking, fear, sweating...
- **Develop a strategy**
  -Treatment team, success plan, therapist...
- **Problem solving approach**
  -Take steps to reduce trigger responses...
- **Emotion focused positive action**
  -Meditation, deep breathing, prayer...
- **Communicate through the trigger**
  -Talk about it, consider solutions together...
- **Trauma specific therapy**
  -CBT, emotion focused therapy...
- **Reasonable thought check**
  -Thoughts based in reality and facts...
- **Trigger warnings**
  -Avoid triggering content, environment...
- **Personal healthcare**
  -Take time to rest, journal, exercise, reset...

WAYS TO DEAL WITH TRIGGERS

POSITIVE | NEGATIVE

- Your partner breaks up with you.
- Your child breaks the television.
- Your boss fires you.
- Your family stops talking to you.
- Your vehicle breaks down.
- A loved one passes away.

- Your partner breaks up with you.
- Your child breaks the television.
- Your boss fires you.
- Your family stops talking to you.
- Your vehicle breaks down.
- A loved one passes away.

EVERYTHING IN OUR LIFE IS AFFECTED BY TRAUMA

We must address our childhood trauma in order to live a healthy, happy, and fulfilled life. Our childhood trauma will continue to grow and build throughout our lives. It will negatively affect and overshadow our thoughts, actions, reactions, friendships, relationships, safety, security, finances, employment, school, learning abilities, and ability to thrive and grow. It shapes our experiences and our reality. We will not be able to see through a factual, non-biased lens until we have addressed our trauma.

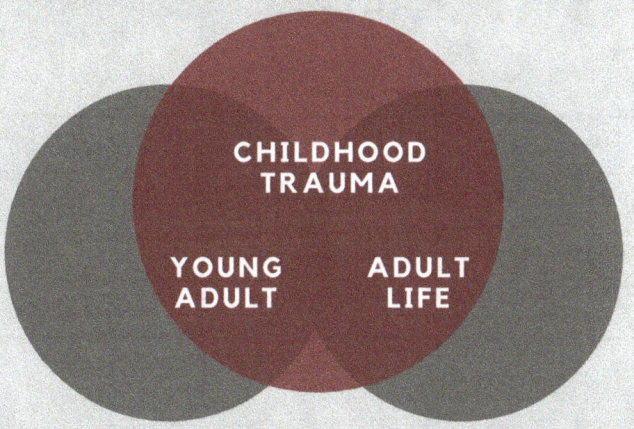

Our childhood trauma plays out in our lives until we are able to address it, resolve it, and heal. Healing doesn't mean that the damage or trauma never existed. It means that the trauma no longer controls our lives.

What we feed will grow. We are not our trauma, pain, or suffering. Traumatic experiences come to us so we can learn from them and grow from them, not accept them as our flawed reality. Trauma is part of the human experience. Trauma allows us to gain strength and resilience.

DECONSTRUCTING TRAUMA | FOUNDATIONAL DEVELOPMENT

NEGATIVE TRAUMA CYCLE

Deconstructing Trauma in our daily lives begins with awareness. **First**, we become aware of the negative results that occur in our daily lives from repeated trauma cycles. **Second**, a Trauma-Informed approach allows us to ask why we are struggling. How can we help meet our needs differently? **And finally**, what are the positive short-term and long-term outcomes of resolving our trauma?

NEGATIVE RESULTS OF MY TRAUMA CYCLE	WHAT IS MY STRUGGLE? WHAT ARE MY UNMET NEEDS?	WHAT NEED IS MET FROM STAYING IN THE TRAUMA CYCLE?	HEALTHY REPLACEMENT THAT MEETS MY NEEDS	HOW RELEASING TRAUMA IMPROVES MY LIFE?
Example: Unhappy and angry at work and home	Lonely and angry	I can control my environment	I can find happiness through a hobby	I can be happier and more positive

THE SIGNIFICANCE OF HABITS

A habit is a learned behavior that becomes reflexive over time. The behavior is often triggered by a certain context. A habit can be healthy, unhealthy, or neutral. A healthy habit might be stretching for ten minutes a day or meditating when you feel stressed. An unhealthy habit could be biting your nails, texting while driving, habitual anger, substance abuse, etc.

Examples of neutral habits include eating the same brand of cereal each morning or taking the same route to work. Unconscious behaviors such as breathing, or blinking do not count as habits because they are instinctive rather than learned.

Habits are important because 40 percent of your actions are not conscious decisions, but habits. Habits are our brain's way of increasing its efficiency. Our brain turns daily actions and behaviors into habits so we can do them automatically, without too much thought or effort, thus freeing up our brainpower for more important challenges.

The power of habits. Create positive change.
Many people have habits that they want to shake off—overeating, smoking, drinking, and substance abuse, for example, are all hard habits to break. People try to quit, but the cravings overwhelm them, and they fall off the wagon.

It's not for lack of determination that they fail. It's lack of understanding of how habits are formed. Negative habits usually begin as an unhealthy coping mechanism that then turns into a constant habit, even when coping is not necessary.

You can start creating new loops and forming new habits that will promote positive changes. It is possible to kick whatever bad habit is holding you back.

DECONSTRUCTING TRAUMA | FOUNDATIONAL DEVELOPMENT

GROWTH OR FIXED MINDSET

Fixed mindsets contribute to goal abandonment; individuals tend to take negative feedback personally because they cannot change it. The growth mindset values skill, commitment, constructive criticism, and resilience for personal improvement. Replace limiting beliefs with empowering ones.

Your mindset can help you achieve goals, overcome trauma cycles, and live a happier, healthier, and more positive life. Changing your perspective can improve your outlook on life and facilitates long-term health and wellbeing. Begin to recognize fixed mindsets in your life that you can change to growth mindsets.

Identify a fixed or growth mindset for each example. Check the correct column. Discuss how to shift the fixed mindsets and the benefits of each growth mindset.

		GROWTH MINDSET	FIXED MINDSET
1.	I'm not good at this.		
2.	I love challenges.		
3.	I don't like it when I make mistakes.		
4.	This is too difficult.		
5.	Practice makes perfect.		
6.	I want to try again.		
7.	When I get frustrated, I reevaluate and try again.		
8.	I can always improve, so I'll keep trying.		
9.	When I fail, I learn.		
10.	I'll never be as smart as her.		

CHANGE YOUR FIXED MINDSETS

Identify and write down five of your fixed mindsets. Then change them into a growth mindset. Discuss how fixed mindsets contribute to repeated negative cycles and the power of positive mindsets.

MY FIXED MINDSETS

1.
2.
3.
4.
5.

MY CHANGE TO GROWTH MINDSET

1.
2.
3.
4.
5.

MANIFEST POSITIVE HABITS IN YOUR LIFE:

1. Examine the Routine – This would be the behavior you want to change. If being an alcoholic is a problem, what makes you do it? What satisfaction do you get?

2. Analyze the Reward – Drinking gives you hangovers and breeds other problems. But you get an immediate reward when you reach for that bottle. Examine the reward. Why do you drink? What is your reward? Is it an escape, the immediate feeling of relaxation or the distraction? Once you know the why of the behavior, it'll be easier to find a better habit that will give you the same reward.

3. Identify the Cue – What compels your behavior? Triggers are stealthy so you might need to observe your own behavior and take notes. What were you doing before an unwanted act? What were you feeling? What reward were you after?

Being aware of the habit and what's reinforcing it is the first step to change.

We tend to focus on negativity. This is a habit as well as a choice. When negativity comes, we can choose to say no and push it away. Like putting a turn signal on when changing lanes, we can shift to the positive. Try the exercise below. You can exhale anything that is bothering you and inhale a positive that you would like to shift to.

SSHI Habit-Breaking Exercise
1. Stretch your arm and hand straight out in a stopping motion; say, "NO" out loud.
2. Place your other hand flat on the center of your chest or belly.
3. Close the eyes, inhale positivity to your body.
4. Exhale negativity out of the mouth like a sigh of relief.
5. Repeat 7 times.

Other options for Inhale & Exhale: Inhale what you need and exhale what you don't.
Inhale: Happiness... Exhale: Sadness — Inhale: Freedom... Exhale: Addiction
Inhale: Confidence... Exhale: Doubt — Inhale: Peace... Exhale: Anger
Inhale: Courage... Exhale: Negativity — Inhale: Joy... Exhale: Grief
Inhale: Resilience... Exhale: Negativity — Inhale: Calm... Exhale: Anxiety
Inhale: Strength... Exhale: Negativity — Inhale: Focus... Exhale: Chaos

DECONSTRUCTING TRAUMA | FOUNDATIONAL DEVELOPMENT

DAILY HABIT TRACKER

TIME MANAGEMENT   m   t   w   t   f   s   s

Early:

On Time:

Late:

MINDSET   m   t   w   t   f   s   s

Positive Mindset:

Neutral Mindset:

Negative Mindset:

GOALS   m   t   w   t   f   s   s

Personal Health Goals:

Recovery Goals:

Family Health Goals:

REST AND RESET   m   t   w   t   f   s   s

Time In Nature

Hobbies

Spiritual Connection

DAILY HABIT TRACKER

	m	t	w	t	f	s	s
_____							
_____							
_____							
_____							

	m	t	w	t	f	s	s
_____							
_____							
_____							
_____							

	m	t	w	t	f	s	s
_____							
_____							
_____							
_____							

	m	t	w	t	f	s	s
_____							
_____							
_____							
_____							

ACTION BRAINSTORM

Brainstorming generates ideas. Brainstorming helps solve basic problems, produce ideas, and address broad issues. Set healthy, suitable, safe, realistic goals, learn from what is not working, figure out why, and then get creative to brainstorm a solution that does work! Doing too much is dangerous. Remember to keep a healthy balance so you are not overwhelmed.

START/DO MORE	KEEP DOING	STOP/DO LESS
Activities that you want start immediately	Activities that you enjoy doing	Activities that you want to stop

HEALTHY REALATIONSHIPS

Healthy relationships with others require work and compromise from both parties, as well as honesty, trust, respect, and open communication. No one is at an unfair disadvantage. Partners treat each other with mutual respect and trust, allowing each to make their own choices without fear of criticism or punishment. Understanding healthy relationships with others is important because it allows us to choose if the relationships in our lives are a good fit. If they are not a good fit for us and are unhealthy, we can begin to determine what steps we need to take to begin to shift these relationships.

Healthy relationships require healthy boundaries for ourselves and others. Consistency between our actions and attitudes is created by setting appropriate boundaries. Establishing boundaries is essential for creating a secure and respectful environment for ourselves. Developing boundaries can have a favorable impact on our self-esteem, thus improving our mood. Aligning our actions and thoughts fosters internal safety and self-respect.

Healthy Relationship with Yourself

Having a healthy relationship with yourself means being able to value yourself as a person and accept your strengths and weaknesses on a daily basis. That consideration includes self-care, self-respect, goodwill, and self-love. It is important to have a healthy relationship with yourself because if you don't the rest of your relationships will not be healthy.

We have to learn how to love ourselves first so we can show the world how we need to be loved.

We cannot expect to be fulfilled and happy through other relationships in our lives if we have not created balance and happiness first inside of ourselves.

DECONSTRUCTING TRAUMA | FOUNDATIONAL DEVELOPMENT

CONFLICT RESOLUTION & DE-ESCALATION

De-Escalation Techniques: A Guide to Conflict Resolution

Conflict is a natural part of human interaction, but effective de-escalation techniques can help manage and resolve conflicts peacefully. Whether in personal relationships, the workplace, or community settings, de-escalation is a valuable skill that promotes understanding and cooperation. Here's a guide to key de-escalation strategies:

1. Stay Calm and Composed: Maintain a calm demeanor to create a conducive environment for resolution. Your composed presence can positively influence the emotional tone of the situation.

2. Active Listening: Listen attentively to the other person's concerns without interrupting. Reflecting back their feelings and thoughts demonstrates empathy and validates their perspective.

3. Empathize: Put yourself in the other person's shoes. Understanding their emotions and acknowledging their viewpoint helps build rapport and fosters a sense of connection.

4. Use Non-Threatening Body Language: Your body language can convey a lot. Maintain open and non-threatening postures to avoid escalating tensions. Make eye contact without staring, and use a calm tone of voice.

5. Mind Your Words: Choose words carefully to avoid aggravating the situation. Use "I" statements to express your feelings and perspective, focusing on your experience rather than blaming the other person.

6. Set Boundaries: Clearly define personal boundaries while remaining respectful. Establishing limits helps prevent further escalation and sets the stage for constructive communication.

7. Identify Common Ground: Find areas of agreement or shared concerns. Highlighting common ground can create a foundation for finding mutually beneficial solutions.

8. Propose Solutions Together: Involve the other person in brainstorming solutions. Collaborative problem-solving empowers both parties and promotes a sense of ownership over the resolution.

9. Take a Time-Out: If emotions are running high, suggest taking a break. A temporary pause allows everyone involved to cool down, gather their thoughts, and approach the situation with a clearer perspective.

10. Seek Mediation: In situations where resolution seems challenging, consider involving a neutral third party to mediate. A mediator can provide an unbiased perspective and guide the conversation towards a positive outcome.

Conclusion:
De-escalation is a powerful tool for resolving conflicts peacefully. By staying calm, listening actively, and employing effective communication strategies, individuals can contribute to creating environments that foster understanding and collaboration. The goal is not to "win" the argument but to find common ground and build strong, safe, and positive relationships.

CONFLICT VS. BENEFIT ANALYSIS

Conflict vs. Benefit
This exercise is about identifying where we are at in our lives. Is it a good fit to accept more? Or is it a better fit to not take on more at that moment? Many things that happen in life, we don't necessarily ask for. For instance, if you are already at capacity in your life, sometimes one more shift or change will throw everything else out of balance. Things come up that we can't avoid, but sometimes it is better to release an idea or a plan than to force things or take on too much.

Mindfulness teaches us that by refraining from doing one thing we are able to prevent another thing from happening. So, with this wisdom and knowledge, we can begin to make balanced choices through a risk analysis thought process. Will adding another task in your life cause conflict and additional stress? Are you able to offer more without causing conflict or chaos? If not, no might be the better option. We tend to offer too much because we care about people and want to help. However, if we are creating conflict in our own lives to help others it is not healthy.

Utilizing this type of explorational thought process in our daily lives opens us to choosing the narrative rather than the narrative choosing us. When we allow ourselves to step back and pause, we can begin to identify what is a good fit, and what is not, through this risk analysis. Diving a little deeper, let's explore what this might look like.

> A conflict vs. benefit mindset is similar to risk vs. reward. Try to examine the consequences before offering or agreeing to something. The outcome for you may be inappropriate and improve someone else's life at your expense. We often want to help people and build our self-worth, but we tend to do too much and get overwhelmed, causing exhaustion and burnout, which compromises our own lives. We are each responsible for our level of happiness and stress.
>
> - Before you offer to do something, ask yourself how it would feel to offer that, and pay attention to the signals your body gives you. If you feel your body drawing back and getting tighter, that means no! We can only fit so many things into one day; consider what you will need to drop if you add something.
>
> - Read the conflict vs. benefit exercise on the following page and list two times you have overcommitted and what you could have done instead. Consider how to be integral with your word for balanced, positive outcomes.

CONFLICT VS. BENEFIT EXERCISE

EXAMPLE—BEFORE YOU COMMIT:

Someone asks you to do something, or they are talking about needing help.

- Before you commit to something, pause. Let them know that you are not sure, but you will get back to them. This gives you time; you don't have to immediately be put on the spot to answer.
- Or, instead of offering right away, you can wait 6-24 hours. Then check in with yourself to see if it's still a good idea on your end to volunteer, and proceed from there. Is it a good fit to add something else to your day? Or will adding one more thing cause chaos and complications for you?

EXAMPLE—AFTER YOU COMMIT:

You've already committed to something but it's not a good fit or you didn't consider the potential consequences, or if an unforeseen complication arises, you'll have to make a decision.

- At this point, you can look to find balance between your actions and keeping the integrity of your word. Use the risk analysis tool to understand what the best action is and how to adjust for optimal balance in your life. Step back and pause to identify what is a good fit and what is not, to avoid unnecessary, unhealthy commitments. We are responsible for our own level of stress.

SITUATION WHERE YOU OVERCOMMITTED:

WHAT YOU COULD HAVE DONE INSTEAD:

SITUATION WHERE YOU OVERCOMMITTED:

WHAT YOU COULD HAVE DONE INSTEAD:

STRESS REDUCTION

Reduce Stress

1. Identify your stressors — The first step to reducing stress is to identify the things that are causing you stress. Once you know what your stressors are, you can begin to work on avoiding or eliminating them.

2. Develop a support system — Another key to reducing stress is to develop a support system. This can include family, friends, or professionals such as therapists or counselors.

3. Exercise regularly — Exercising is a great way to reduce stress. It helps to release endorphins, which have mood-boosting effects.

4. Practice relaxation techniques — There are many different relaxation techniques that can be effective in reducing stress. Some examples include deep breathing, meditation, and yog

5. Be Alone — Five minutes of alone time can help you collect your thoughts and clear your head.

Make holistic lifestyle changes — Holistic means tending the whole person. Balancing the 8 Dimensions of Wellness incluce emotional, financial, social, spiritual, occupational, physical, intellectual, and environmental aspects of our lives. Making lifestyle changes, such as eating a healthy diet, getting enough sleep, and reducing alcohol consumption, can also help reduce stress levels. Set boundaries between work and personal time. Don't try to do everything yourself. Delegate tasks to others and ask for help when you need it.

Personal Care

1. Eat Well — Make sure to eat a variety of nutritious foods that provide your body with the necessary vitamins and minerals.

2. Keep the Body Moving — Just 30 minutes of walking every day can help boost your mood and improve your health.

3. Get Enough Sleep — Aim for 7-9 hours of quality sleep each night. A good night's sleep is essential for your body's recovery and mental health.

4. Manage Stress — Implement stress management techniques such as meditation, deep breathing exercises, yoga, or journaling.

5. Set and Pursue Goals — Have goals and aspirations that give your life purpose and direction. Achieving small milestones can boost your self-esteem and sense of accomplishment.

DECONSTRUCTING TRAUMA | FOUNDATIONAL DEVELOPMENT

Embodying Grace

Grace is what emerges from the struggle... Grace is the courage to face the uncomfortable

Grace is our true raw self exposed. Not only in spite of but because of our flaws, this is how we learn. Grace allows us to take our struggles, our trials, our lessons and turn them into wisdom.

Through this Grace, we know we are not our trauma, we are not our suffering, we learn our lessons and move on. Grace allows us to separate negative feelings, triggers, and experiences from our identity.

Grace knows the struggle is real but allows us to release the struggle. We are not the struggle, we are not the pain, we are not the suffering. We are not alone.

Grace is humility in action; humility is not shame.

Being humble takes courage, strength, balance, and Grace.

Grace allows us to support and love others without controlling, manipulating, or running their lives.

Grace allows us to evolve from our trauma.

Grace allows us to let others walk their own journey, without rushing in fixing, saving, and taking away their opportunity for lessons and growth.

Grace allows us to trust others to handle their own journey, not in the way we see fit but in the way that is best served for them. They will learn their lesson... or they won't; this is not up to us. It is our responsibility to be mindful and care for ourselves by removing ourselves from unhealthy situations. It is not our responsibility to change anyone else or make them see the light.

Grace allows us to release this to a higher space, a higher presence. In this way, we learn not to take situations personally.

Grace tells us it's not always about us...What a relief!

Grace allows us to fully and completely love and accept ourselves at the most basic fundamental level.

Grace is our true self realized. Our true self is Love, Light, and Grace.

Grace Embodied...Is You.

Renee Spiritflyer Frye 2022

EMBODYING GRACE

The Embodying Grace poem contains many helpful teachings, to help us stay balanced and in our own lane. Check True or False below.

FALSE / **TRUE**

- ☐ ☐ GRACE IS THE COURAGE FACE THE UNCOMFORTABLE.
- ☐ ☐ GRACE ALLOWS US TO SEPARATE OUR EXPERIENCES FROM OUR IDENTITY.
- ☐ ☐ THE STRUGGLE IS NOT REAL.
- ☐ ☐ HUMILITY IS NOT SHAME.
- ☐ ☐ GRACE IS CONTROLLING OTHERS.
- ☐ ☐ GRACE ALLOWS US EVOLVE FROM OUR TRAUMA.
- ☐ ☐ GRACE IS TAKING OTHER PEOPLES LESSONS.
- ☐ ☐ WE ARE RESPONSIBLE FOR REMOVING OURSELVES FROM UNHEALTHY SITUATIONS.
- ☐ ☐ IT IS OUR RESPONSIBILITY TO MAKE OTHERS SEE THE LIGHT.
- ☐ ☐ GRACE ALLOWS US TO NOT TAKE SITUATIONS PERSONALLY.
- ☐ ☐ GRACE ALLOWS US TO FULLY LOVE OURSELVES.
- ☐ ☐ WE ARE LOVE, LIGHT, AND GRACE.

WELLNESS CHECK

Our recovery wellness is based on our overall wellness. If your needs are met, you will not need to use substances.

Rate the following

PHYSICAL

	Never	Rarely	Sometimes	Always
I feel good about my body	○	○	○	○
I exercise to keep my body healthy	○	○	○	○
I get 7-8 hours of sleep every day	○	○	○	○
I include nutritious food in my diet	○	○	○	○
I spend time in nature	○	○	○	○

EMOTIONAL

	Never	Rarely	Sometimes	Always
I can manage my feelings appropriately	○	○	○	○
I am able to cope when stress	○	○	○	○
I have a positive outlook and energy	○	○	○	○
I allot time for my hobbies	○	○	○	○

SPIRITUAL

	Never	Rarely	Sometimes	Always
I have a spiritual connection	○	○	○	○
I connect with a spiritual community	○	○	○	○
I have a belief that gives me hope	○	○	○	○
I feel spiritually healthy	○	○	○	○

Your Healthy Wellness Routine

CHECKLIST

Physical activities for the week

- ☐ Exercise and/or go for a walk
- ☐ Eat healthy food and snacks
- ☐ Get 7 hours of sleep per night
- ☐ Enjoy stillness and/or meditate
- ☐ Spend time in nature

Mental, emotional, and spiritual activities for the week

- ☐ Journal
- ☐ Listen to favorite music
- ☐ Spend time with family/friends
- ☐ Practice meditation
- ☐ Spiritual connection
- ☐ Do something fun

A wellness plan is a program that offers tools, guidelines, and resources to boost health and well-being. A wellness plan can greatly improve our chances of producing positive change and successful habits. When we focus on communication skills, social skills, and self-management skills, we are able to strengthen our vulnerabilities by changing triggers and reinforcing a positive environment.

We have a better chance of success when we recognize issues, establish a plan, put it into action, and then check in to evaluate where we are at accountability. Wellness plans are important because life is challenging! We have to actively participate in creating and bringing positivity into our lives to manifest desired results!

DAILY PERSONAL HEALTH

DATE ___ /___ /___

S M T W T F S

CHECKLIST

- ○ MAKE YOUR BED
- ○ TAKE YOUR MEDICATIONS & VITAMINS
- ○ SKINCARE ROUTINE
- ○ HEALTHY MEALS & NEW RECIPE
- ○ GO FOR A WALK OR HIKE
- ○ CLEAN HOUSE
- ○ WASH CLOTHES
- ○ LISTEN TO MUSIC
- ○ TAKE A POWER NAP
- ○ SOCIAL MEDIA BREAK

- ○ TAKE A LONG BATH
- ○ DO A FACE MASK
- ○ CALL A FRIEND OR FAMILY
- ○ MEDITATION
- ○ WATCH A MOVIE
- ○ CUDDLE A PET OR HUMAN
- ○ TRY A NEW RESTAURANT
- ○ MAKE TIME TO READ
- ○ TRY A NEW RECIPE
- ○ NO PHONE 30 MINS BEFORE BED

WORKOUT

- ○ CARDIO
- ○ WEIGHT
- ○ YOGA
- ○ STRETCH
- ○ REST DAY
- ○ OTHER

HOURS OF SLEEP (Hours)

🌙 🌙 🌙 🌙 🌙 🌙 🌙 🌙
1 2 3 4 5 6 7 8

WATER BALANCE (Glass)

1 2 3 4 5 6 7 8

THINGS THAT MAKE ME HAPPY TODAY

MOOD

ANGRY TIRED SAD GREAT FUN

DECONSTRUCTING TRAUMA | FOUNDATIONAL DEVELOPMENT

DAILY REFLECTION

Date: _____

1. How did I feel today?
   _____
   _____
   _____
   _____

2. Three great things that happened today:
   ✦ _____
   _____

   ✦ _____
   _____

   ✦ _____
   _____

3. Challenges of the day:
   _____
   _____
   _____
   _____

4. Achievements of the day:
   _____
   _____
   _____
   _____

5. I am grateful for:
   _____
   _____
   _____
   _____

6. What can I do to make tomorrow better than today?
   _____
   _____
   _____
   _____

GOAL SETTING

GOALS
Goals work best when they are specific, measurable, achievable, relevant, and time-bound.

BENEFITS
List the benefits you expect to gain from achieving this goal. This will be a constant reminder of why you're working toward it.

OBSTACLES
With non-judgemental mindset. Identify potential obstacles or challenges that may arise during your journey.

RESOURCES
Determine the resources you'll need to achieve your goal. This includes financial resources, time, skills, or other necessary assets.

ACTION STEPS
Break your goal down into actionable steps or milestones. You need to complete these smaller tasks to reach your goal.

TIMELINE
Create a timeline for each action step. Specify when you plan to complete each task, which will help you stay on track.

REVIEW
Review the previous goal periods to analyse successes and areas in which to improve.

CELEBRATE WINS
Acknowledge and celebrate what you've achieved in the previous goal period.

MIND MAP
Mind map, using a visual display of ideas, thoughts, or concepts to track development and set long- and short-term goals.

BREAK IT DOWN
Break down goals into annual and quarterly periods to identify next steps for 90 days.

NEXT 90 DAYS
Define the tasks and sub-goals you'll need to complete to reach the goal in 90 days.

CHECK-IN
Implement your plan. Check-in daily & weekly to identify successes and challenges.

2 WEEK BLOCKS SUGGESTION: Try working 2 weeks at a time. This will reduce stress and assist short-term goals that lead to long-term goals, as well as increase productivity and ease in reaching your goals.

DECONSTRUCTING TRAUMA | FOUNDATIONAL DEVELOPMENT

GOAL SETTING

- GOALS
- ↓
- BENEFITS
- ↓
- OBSTACLES
- ↓
- RESOURCES
- ↓
- ACTION STEPS
- ↓
- TIMELINE

- REVIEW
- ↓
- CELEBRATE WINS
- ↓
- MIND MAP
- ↓
- BREAK IT DOWN
- ↓
- NEXT 14 DAYS
- ↓
- CHECK-IN

2 WEEK BLOCKS SUGGESTION: Try working 2 weeks at a time. This will reduce stress and assist short-term goals that lead to long-term goals, as well as increase productivity and ease in reaching your goals.

DECONSTRUCTING TRAUMA | FOUNDATIONAL DEVELOPMENT

Wellness Long-Term Success Plan

Broader plan. Long-term lifestyle changes and maintenance plans. List the steps in your long-term wellness success plan.

- _____
  _____
  _____
  _____

- _____
  _____
  _____
  _____

- _____
  _____
  _____
  _____

- _____
  _____
  _____
  _____

- _____
  _____
  _____
  _____

Wellness Short-Term Success Plan

Short, immediate plan. Short-term, fluid steps that will take you to the long-term plan. List the steps in your long-term wellness success plan.

- _____
  _____
  _____
  _____
  _____

- _____
  _____
  _____
  _____
  _____

- _____
  _____
  _____
  _____
  _____

- _____
  _____
  _____
  _____
  _____

- _____
  _____
  _____
  _____
  _____

SETTING YOUR GOALS

When we are focused on negativity and chaos, our reality becomes altered, creating experiences where we don't have the ability to reach the goals we've set for ourselves. This leads to depression, low self value, hopelessness, and addiction. The first step to developing a positive outlook is having long-term and short-term goals. Motivate yourself to achieve them with a constant stream of positivity. Refuse to allow negativity into your mind. As you complete your goals, you'll start to see a snowball effect. Setting realistic short-term goals will lead to successful long-term goals and a positive growth mindset.

90 DAYS

ACTION PLAN
-
-
-
-

60 DAYS

ACTION PLAN
-
-
-
-

30 DAYS

ACTION PLAN
-
-
-
-

Walk in Beauty

One of our biggest teachings is learning to "Walk in Beauty" daily, in the world around us as well as in the world inside of us. It requires moral, spiritual, physical, mental, and emotional endurance, integrity, commitment, and patience. "Walking in Beauty" is an intentional life journey; it is a way of life that takes work and dedication. It is not easy, but it is simple.

Many times, life complications will unwind on their own when we are not feeding them with an exhausted, frantic negative mindset. We do not have to become stressed or exhausted to fix what is not working.

The Deconstructing Trauma program teaches us how to "Walk in Beauty," utilizing social development life skills and tools that allow us to step back from the challenges and not take them personally. We do not ignore the challenges, but rather choose a mindset of peace and openness, appreciating the lessons and moving through them, rather than feeding the negativity around them.

These lessons are how we grow in mind, body, and spirit. We have been given the gift of knowledge; if we are able to process, learn, and use this knowledge, it will manifest as wisdom that we can use in our lives. This is how we learn to "Walk in Beauty".

"Walking in Beauty" is challenging, but it is how we live our best life. "Walking in Beauty" doesn't mean that everything is perfect. It means we get to choose how we show up in the world. How we live our best lives, reflecting beauty, grace, strength, light, compassion, resilience, peace, respect, kindness, balance, joy, and love, daily for ourselves and others.

"Walking in Beauty" is the human challenge; it reminds us and teaches us how to respect the sacred hoop of life and all that resides within it. The earth, the elements, the people, and the animals. How can you apply "Walking in Beauty" to your daily life? It is a continual dance filled with highs and lows. You are the medicine; you are the beauty; allow your heart to guide you on this journey to self. You are the miracle you've been looking for, "Walk in Beauty."

2023 - Renee Frye

SUPPORT CONTACT LIST

NAME :
ADDRESS :
PHONE :
EMAIL :
NOTES :

NAME :
ADDRESS :
PHONE :
EMAIL :
NOTES :

NAME :
ADDRESS :
PHONE :
EMAIL :
NOTES :

NAME :
ADDRESS :
PHONE :
EMAIL :
NOTES :

NAME :
ADDRESS :
PHONE :
EMAIL :
NOTES :

NAME :
ADDRESS :
PHONE :
EMAIL :
NOTES :

NAME :
ADDRESS :
PHONE :
EMAIL :
NOTES :

NAME :
ADDRESS :
PHONE :
EMAIL :
NOTES :

LIST OF RESOURCES

01. SACRED SOL HEALING INSTITUTE (SSHI)

SSHI. https://sacredsolhealing.com/
We are a peer-run organization that provides holistic mental wellness and substance abuse recovery support resources. We provide a healing-centered approach, meeting each person where they are at, offering hope, education, and life wellness support.

02. NATIONAL ALLIANCE ON MENTAL ILLNESS (NAMI)

NAMI. https://www.nami.org/Home
NAMI HelpLine is available M-F 10 am – 10 pm, ET. Connect by phone 800-950-6264 or text "Helpline" to 62640, or chat. In a crisis call or text 988.* NAMI, the National Alliance on Mental Illness, is the nation's largest grassroots mental health organization dedicated to building better lives for the millions of Americans affected by mental illness.

03. SUICIDE PREVENTION

988 Suicide & Crisis Lifeline. https://988lifeline.org/
We can all help prevent suicide. The 988 Lifeline provides 24/7, free and confidential support for people in distress, prevention and crisis resources for you or your loved ones, and best practices for professionals in the United States.
Suicide Prevention Resource Center. https://sprc.org/

04. YOUR LOCAL MEDICAL AND MENTAL HEALTH PROVIDERS

Online: Search "Medical and mental health providers near me."

CLOSING THOUGHTS:

As we live through challenging life experiences, we are meant to learn and evolve. We do not have to suffer to surrender to lessons. We can surrender the suffering.

We can live happy, healthy lives, free of addiction and past trauma, through a trauma-responsive wellness approach. We are not our trauma; it is a challenge for us to learn from and grow.

YOU ARE SPECIAL, YOU ARE VALUABLE, YOU ARE LOVED, YOU ARE MORE THAN ENOUGH.

YOU ARE WHOLE, YOU ARE FREE,
YOU ALWAYS HAVE BEEN, AND YOU ALWAYS WILL BE. HERE WE PEEL BACK THE LAYERS TO ACCESS THAT SPACE. EVERYTHING YOU NEED IS CONTAINED WITHIN.

www.ingramcontent.com/pod-product-compliance
Lightning Source LLC
LaVergne TN
LVHW081539070526
838199LV00056B/3718

9798989654895